Green Anaconda

The World's Heaviest Snake

by Molly Smith

Consultant: Meredith Whitney
Herpetology and Conservation Manager
The Maryland Zoo in Baltimore
Baltimore, MD

BEARPORT
PUBLISHING

New York, New York

Credits

Cover, ©Joe McDonald/Corbis; 2–3, ©Ed Degginger/www.color-pic.com; 4, Kathrin Ayer; 4–5, ©DDP-Jens Ulrich Koch/Agence France-Presse/Getty Images; 6, ©Brian Kenney/Getty Images; 7BKG, ©Brian Kenney/Getty Images; 8, ©Mark Bowler/NHPA; 9, ©Tom Brakefield/Corbis; 10, ©McDonald Wildlife Photography; 11, ©McDonald Wildlife Photography; 12, ©BIOS/Klein & Hubert/Peter Arnold; 13, ©Bill Love/NHPA; 14, ©Erwin & Peggy Bauer/Peter Arnold; 15, ©BIOS/Crocetta Tony/Peter Arnold; 16–17, ©Erwin & Peggy Bauer/Peter Arnold; 18, ©Jany Savaunet/Photo Researchers; 19, ©Keystone/Sandro Campardo/AP; 20, ©Joel Creed/Ecoscene Corbis; 21, ©David Northcott/Corbis; 22L, ©Bill Love/NHPA; 22C, ©Daniel Heuclin/NHPA; 22R, ©Anthony Bannister/NHPA; 23TL, ©Claudine Laabs/Photo Researchers; 23TR, ©Guido Cozzi/Atlantide Photo Travel/Corbis; 23BL, ©Keystone/Sandro Campardo/AP; 23BR, ©McDonald Wildlife Photography; 23BKG, ©Robert Pickett/Corbis.

Publisher: Kenn Goin
Senior Editor: Lisa Wiseman
Editorial Development: Nancy Hall, Inc.
Creative Director: Spencer Brinker
Photo Researcher: Carousel Research, Inc.: Mary Teresa Giancoli
Design: Otto Carbajal

Library of Congress Cataloging-in-Publication Data

Smith, Molly, 1974-
 Green anaconda : the world's heaviest snake / by Molly Smith.
    p. cm. — (Supersized!)
 Includes bibliographical references (p.   ) and index.
 ISBN-13: 978-1-59716-391-0 (lib. bdg.)
 ISBN-10: 1-59716-391-0 (lib. bdg.)
 1. Anaconda—Juvenile literature. I. Title.

QL666.O63S65 2007
597.96'7—dc22

                        2006028815

For more information, write to Bearport Publishing Company, Inc., 101 Fifth Avenue, Suite 6R, New York, New York 10003. Printed in the United States of America.

10 9 8 7 6 5 4 3 2

Contents

A Green Giant

The green anaconda is the heaviest snake in the world.

Some snakes may be longer, but no other snake weighs as much.

A green anaconda is heavier than an adult male lion.

Green anacondas can weigh more than 500 pounds (227 kg). They can grow up to 30 feet (9 m) long.

At Home

Green anacondas live in the Amazon **rain forest** in South America.

These snakes spend much of their lives in water.

Green anacondas can also be found in caves and trees that are near water.

Green Anacondas in the Wild

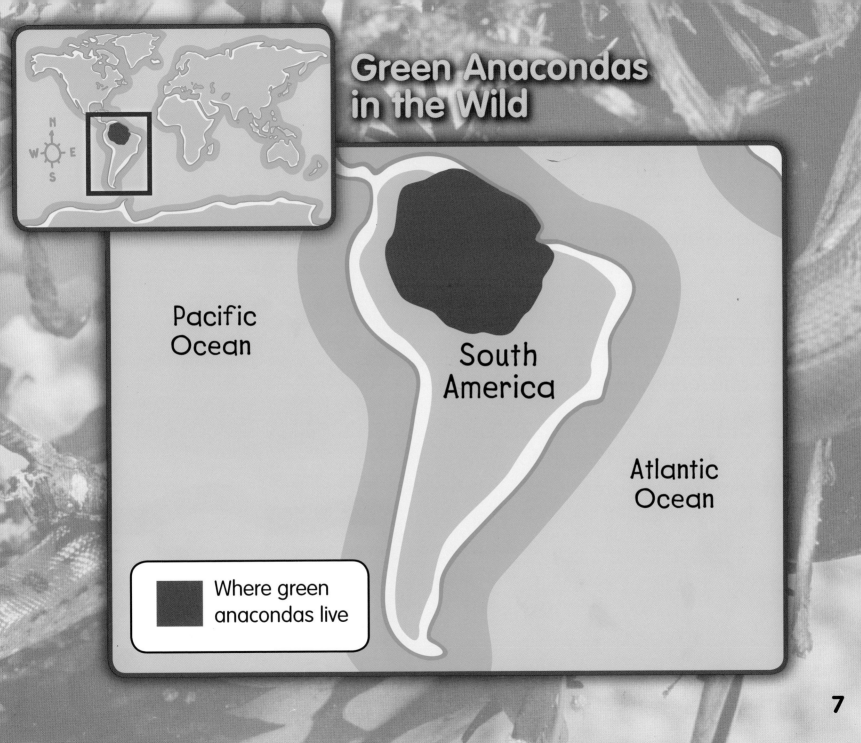

Pacific Ocean

South America

Atlantic Ocean

Where green anacondas live

Fast Swimmers

Green anacondas move slowly on land.

Yet these snakes move quickly and smoothly in water.

Green anacondas can even swim underwater.

They can hold their breath for more than ten minutes.

nostril

eye

An anaconda's eyes and nostrils are on top of its head. This position lets the snake see and breathe while the rest of its body is underwater.

Where Are They?

Green anacondas have dark green **scales** that are covered with black spots.

Some spots have yellow centers.

These colors help the snakes hide.

Other animals cannot spot them among the green plants or in the dark water.

scales

Each green anaconda has its own pattern of scales under its body. No two patterns look the same.

Hunting by Surprise

While hunting, a green anaconda hides in water or hangs in a tree.

The snake waits for an animal to come close.

Then it snatches the animal with its sharp teeth.

A green anaconda always catches its food by surprise.

capybara

Green anacondas eat **capybaras**, fish, birds, and reptiles.

12

The Big Squeeze

A green anaconda kills by squeezing.

It wraps its long body around an animal.

Soon the animal can't breathe.

Then the anaconda opens its wide jaws and swallows the animal whole.

Sometimes anacondas drown the animals they catch.

A Full Belly

After a green anaconda eats, it rests for several days.

It needs to let the food break down in its stomach.

The snake will not have to eat again for a long time.

Anacondas can go as long as six months between meals.

17

Little Snakes

Female green anacondas give birth to between 20 and 40 live babies.

Sometimes they have up to 100 babies!

The young anacondas have many enemies.

Wild cats, giant otters, and **caimans** hunt the little snakes.

caiman

Anacondas do not lay eggs as most snakes do. They give birth to live babies.

 Growing Up

From birth, anacondas can care for themselves.

They grow quickly until they are about three years old.

Then they grow more slowly for many years.

Green anacondas need a lot of time to become the world's heaviest snake!

Anacondas live for about 15 to 20 years in the wild. They can live up to 30 years in zoos.

More Heavy Snakes

Anacondas, like all snakes, belong to a group of animals called reptiles. Most reptiles hatch from eggs. Reptiles are cold-blooded and are covered with scales.

Here are three more heavy snakes.

Reticulated Python

The reticulated python is the longest snake in the world. It can weigh more than 300 pounds (136 kg).

King Cobra

The king cobra can weigh up to 20 pounds (9 kg).

Puff Adder

The puff adder can weigh more than 13 pounds (5.8 kg).

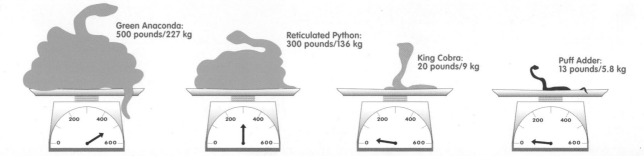

Green Anaconda: 500 pounds/227 kg

Reticulated Python: 300 pounds/136 kg

King Cobra: 20 pounds/9 kg

Puff Adder: 13 pounds/5.8 kg

Glossary

caimans
(CAY-monz)
reptiles in the
alligator family
living in Central
and South America

rain forest
(RAYN FOR-ist)
large area of land
covered with trees
and plants, where
lots of rain falls

capybaras
(ka-pee-BAR-uhz)
large rat-like
animals that live in
South America

scales (SKALEZ)
small, thin
plate-like parts
that cover a
reptile or fish

Index

Read More

George, Linda. *Anacondas.* Mankato, MN: Capstone Press (2001).

Steele, Christy. *Anacondas.* Austin, TX: Steck-Vaughn (2001).

Weber, Valerie J. *Anacondas: World's Largest Snakes.* Milwaukee, WI: Gareth Stevens Publishing (2002).

Learn More Online

To learn more about green anacondas, visit **www.bearportpublishing.com/SuperSized**